faith first

Legacy Edition

Additional Activities

A Blackline Master Book
with Answer Key

Grade Four

Marilyn Peters Krawczyk
Dee Ready

RESOURCES FOR CHRISTIAN LIVING®

www.FaithFirst.com

NIHIL OBSTAT
Rev. Msgr. Robert M. Coerver
Censor Librorum

IMPRIMATUR
† Most Rev. Charles V. Grahmann
Bishop of Dallas

June 27, 2005

The Nihil Obstat and Imprimatur are official declarations that the material reviewed is free of doctrinal or moral error. No implication is contained therein that those granting the Nihil Obstat and Imprimatur agree with the contents, opinions, or statements expressed.

Acknowledgements

Scripture excerpts are based on the *New American Bible with Revised New Testament and Psalms* copyright © 1991, 1986, 1970, Confraternity of Christian Doctrine, Washington, DC. Used with permission. All rights reserved. No part of the *New American Bible* may be reproduced by any means without the permission of the copyright owner.

Send all inquiries to:
RCL • Resources for Christian Living
200 East Bethany Drive
Allen, Texas 75002-3804

Toll Free   877-275-4725
Fax   800-688-8356

Visit us at **www.RCLweb.com**
            www.faithfirst.com

Printed in the United States of America

20494   ISBN 0-7829-1090-4

1 2 3 4 5 6 7 8 9 10
05 06 07 08 09 10

Contents

Introduction

One of the guiding principles of the *Faith First Legacy* program is that we want students to understand the faith of the Catholic Church and how to live out that faith in everyday life. The *Faith First Legacy Additional Activities* extend the faith knowledge of the children. The activities invite the students to think, reflect, and integrate the faith of the Church into their lives. They might do these activities alone, with groups in class, or at home. Versatility of use was a key element in writing and designing the activities. These engaging activities may be used anytime, anywhere—it's up to you.

Growing as a person of faith includes learning to look at one's actions and the world in a different way—in a faith-filled way. When we see things through the prism of faith, all is changed. The *Faith First Legacy Additional Activities* help to polish that prism, enriching the students and their world.

God bless you in your work, and have a great year!

Name _____

We Find a Message of Faith

We show our faith in God in many ways.

Color in the squares to find what one Apostle said to show his faith. Color all the squares that contain the following letters: B, E, F, H, I, J, K, P, Q, S, T, V, W, X, Z.

Thomas's Message of Faith

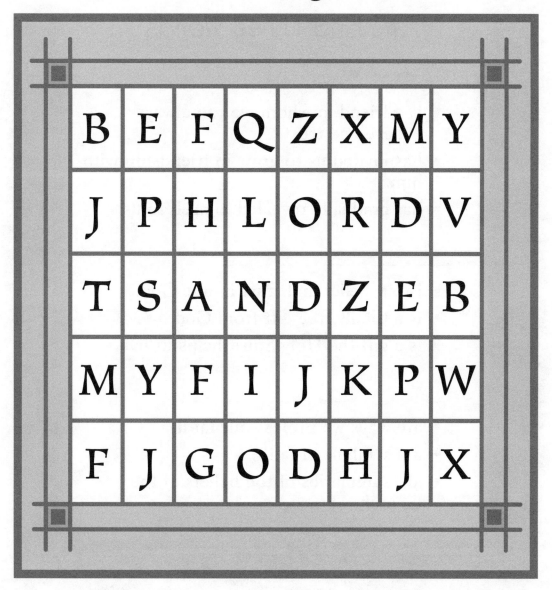

B	E	F	Q	Z	X	M	Y
J	P	H	L	O	R	D	V
T	S	A	N	D	Z	E	B
M	Y	F	I	J	K	P	W
F	J	G	O	D	H	J	X

We Believe That God Will Always Be with Us

God has told us that he will always be with us.
The Bible and Jesus tell us this, too.

Use the clues on this page to find out more about our faith.

We Find Three Words

1. __ ___ ___

   - is a friend in whom we can always believe and trust.
   - has invited us to grow in friendship with him.
   - has gradually revealed himself to us.

2. __ __ __ __ __

   - is our belief and trust in one God.
   - is a totally free gift from God.
   - is a gift the Holy Spirit helps us live.

3. __ __ __ __ __ __

   - are ways we profess our faith.
   - are symbols of faith.
   - are summaries of the beliefs of the Church.

Name _____

We Learn about the Covenant

The Bible tells us about the Covenant God made
with the Israelites. He promised to be faithful
to them. They promised to follow his laws.

Fill in the missing vowels: a, e, i, o, u.

Discover how the Israelites felt about God's laws.

The People's Promise

"__v__ryth__ng   th__

L__rd   h__s   s__ __d,

w__   w__ll   d__."

Clue: see Exodus 19:8

We Make a Bookmark for Our Bible

When we read the Bible, we learn about God. Try to read the Bible often.

1. Make a Bible bookmark.

2. On it, draw symbols that remind you of the Bible.

3. Use your bookmark to help you find the place where you are reading.

We Unscramble Words from a Bible Story

We read the story of Hannah, Samuel, and Eli in the Old Testament. This story tells us that God speaks to us and asks us to listen to him.

Unscramble the words about people, places, and things in the Bible story. Then choose one word and write three sentences about it.

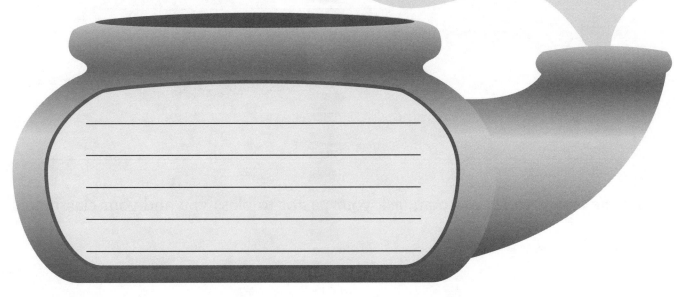

Bible Story Words

1. nHanah
2. lemuaS
3. erhSni
4. ersilaestI
5. krA fo eht venConta

6. Shhoil
7. sedJug
8. ldO mensTatet
9. amerJulse
10. emTpel

Name _____

We Invite Our Pastor to Talk to Us

Eli was a priest who served God's people. Samuel served them too as a judge. Like Eli and Samuel, your pastor serves others. He serves the Church. Invite him to your class or group to share with you some things he does for others. Follow the steps below for his visit.

With your classmates make a welcome sign, banner, or card for your pastor.

When he visits your classroom, ask him questions such as the ones below. Write one more question to ask your pastor.

- How did you become pastor of our parish?

- What do you like best about being a pastor?

- What is the most difficult thing about being a pastor?

- What message do you want to share with us today?

-

Before he leaves your classroom, ask your pastor to bless you and your classmates.

We Make a Rhyming Poem about Creation

Think of all that is beautiful and wonderful in our world. God created all of this. Now write a rhyming poem about something wonderful in creation. Or write about many wonderful things! Make your poem at least two lines long. Here is an example of a poem about creation:

Zebras prance! Flowers dance!
Snow flakes! Bread bakes!
Rains fall! Friends call!
Birds nest! We rest!

We Become Stewards of God's Creation

God asks us to take care of his wonderful world.
He asks us to become caregivers, or stewards, of
creation.

Complete each statement below to show how you
take care of God's world.

I Am a Steward of God's Creation

1. I recycle and reuse materials when I _____
   _____.

2. I care for growing things, plants, trees, and flowers when I _____
   _____.

3. I keep the air and water clean when I _____
   _____.

4. I care for God's creatures, including my pets, when I _____
   _____.

Name _____

We Discover a Promise God Made

We read about the prophet Isaiah in the Bible. God spoke to us through Isaiah. God gave us a message of hope and love.

We have circled the first letter in the series of letters below. To find God's message, circle every third letter after the first circled letter. Write God's message in the spaces below.

God's Promise

Ⓜ N Q Y / B P L R D O N S V D A E /
C M S V W H F D A G N L Z Y L /
R S N J R E F T V O B E A J R /
M D L U Q E N P A S R V K G E /
O X Y C B O M A U .

Clue: see Isaiah 54:10.

<u>M</u> __ __ __ __ __

__ __ __ __ __

__ __ __ __ __ __

__ __ __ __ __ __ __ __ __ .

We Know That God Answers Our Prayers

The Bible tells us that God answered the prayers of his people. God promised a savior. God sent his only Son, Jesus, to be our Savior.

Think of a time when God answered your prayer. Then draw a three-picture storyboard with speech bubbles. Show your prayer being answered.

We Know That Jesus Wants Us to Have Faith

Jesus teaches us about God's love. He heals those who have faith.

Use the dot detector below to discover what Jesus says to those he heals. Start with the first column. Then go across from left to right, copying the letters on the lines below. The first letter has been done for you.

Jesus' Message

"L _ _   _ _   _ _

_ _ _ _   _ _ _   _ _ _

_ _ _ _ _ _ _ _ _ _

_ _ _ _   _ _ _ _ _ "

Clue: see Matthew 9:29

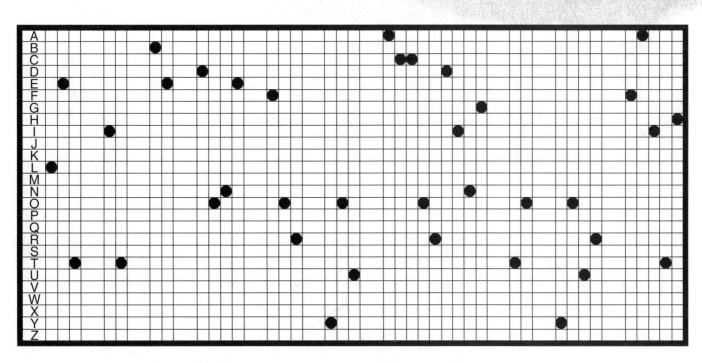

We Celebrate Our Baptism!

Jesus began his ministry when John the Baptist baptized him in the Jordan River. Your own Baptism was one of the most important days of your life! On that day, you became a follower of Jesus.

Celebrate your Baptism by filling in the blanks below. Then color the border. If necessary, ask your parents for help in filling in the blanks.

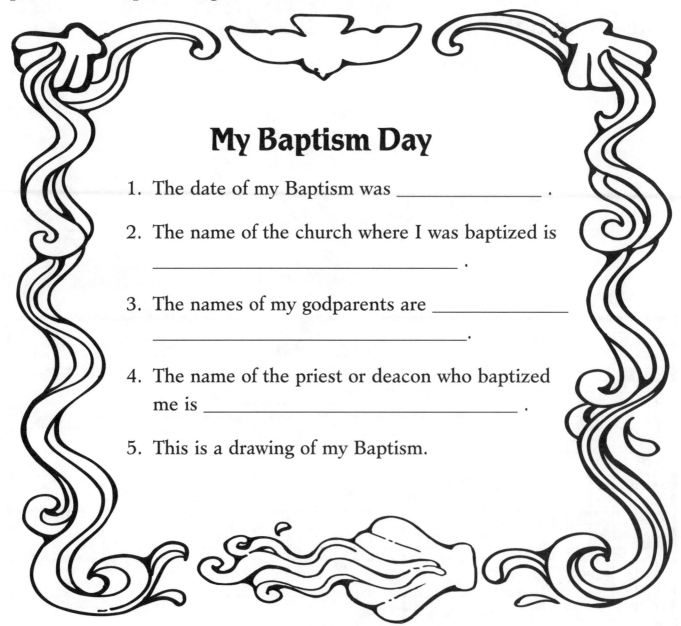

My Baptism Day

1. The date of my Baptism was _____ .

2. The name of the church where I was baptized is _____ .

3. The names of my godparents are _____ _____ .

4. The name of the priest or deacon who baptized me is _____ .

5. This is a drawing of my Baptism.

We Put Events in Jesus' Life in the Order They Happened

Jesus spent his public life teaching us about God's love.

The Bible tells us many things about what Jesus said and did. Look at the following events in the last days of Jesus' life on earth. Place these events in the order in which they happened.

The Last Days of Jesus on Earth

a. Jesus prays in the Garden of Gethsemane.

b. Jesus hangs on the cross for three hours.

c. Jesus is raised from the dead.

d. Jesus ascends into heaven forty days after his Resurrection.

e. Jesus enters Jerusalem in triumph on the Sunday before he died.

f. Jesus is placed in a tomb after his death.

g. Jesus carries his cross to Calvary.

h. Jesus celebrates the Passover meal with his disciples.

i. Jesus appears to his followers after his Resurrection.

j. Jesus dies on the cross.

Here is the order of the events in Jesus' life:

___ ___ ___ ___ ___ ___ ___ ___ ___ ___

1   2   3   4   5   6   7   8   9   10

We Write a Letter about Jesus' Forgiveness

Jesus hung on a cross for three hours. His enemies made fun of him. But Jesus forgave them and said, "Father, forgive them, they do not know what they do" (based on Luke 23:34).

Imagine that you are among the people standing by the cross. Jesus' enemies laugh at him. They make fun of him. Then you hear his words of forgiveness. Write a letter to someone who lives far away from Jerusalem. Tell this person how you feel about Jesus.

We Write a Play About Pentecost

Forty days after Easter, Jesus returned to his Father. His disciples and Mary went back to Jerusalem to wait for the coming of the Holy Spirit.

Imagine that you are with Mary and Jesus' disciples. You are in an upper room waiting for the gift of the Holy Spirit. What are you feeling?

Next imagine that the Holy Spirit comes! What do you see? How do you feel?

Then imagine you go outside with Peter and talk to the crowds. What do you see? How do you feel? What do you do next?

With a partner or a group, write a three-act play about Pentecost.

- In Act 1 show the disciples and Mary waiting for the Holy Spirit to come.

- In Act 2 show the Holy Spirit coming.

- In Act 3 show what happens after the Holy Spirit comes.

Create roles for several classmates. Think about using a narrator to tell part of the story.

Write dialogue for your characters to say. With this dialogue show what each character in the play is feeling and thinking.

Write stage directions too. Then the actors will know what hand gestures, facial expressions, and body movements they should use.

Finally, collect props, such as clothing, that the actors can use to make your play seem more real.

With the help of some of your classmates, perform your play for your school or parish.

We Solve a Pentecost Crossword Puzzle

The Holy Spirit is our helper and teacher. Ask the Holy Spirit to help you solve the following crossword puzzle.

Our Pentecost Crossword Puzzle

Across

2. The Holy Spirit came to the disciples and Mary on _____.

4. The Holy Spirit came like a mighty _____.

5. The third Person of the Trinity is the Holy _____.

7. When the Holy Spirit came, tongues of _____ appeared.

8. Fire and wind are _____ in the Pentecost story. They help us understand what we cannot see.

11. The Holy Spirit helped the disciples invite others to have _____ in Jesus.

Down

1. _____ promised to send the Holy Spirit.

3. The mystery of one God in three divine Persons is the Holy _____.

6. Jesus _____ to send the Holy Spirit.

9. We believe in three Persons in one _____.

10. The Holy Spirit pardons us and fills us with _____.

We Unscramble Words About a Bible Story

Jesus told us the story of the good shepherd who cares for his sheep. Jesus is the Good Shepherd. We are Jesus' sheep; he cares for us. The Church asks us to care for others too. We do this when we live the Corporal Works of Mercy.

Look at the words in the Word Bank. Find the words in the block of letters. They may be horizontal, vertical, diagonal, backward, or forward. Circle each word when you find it.

Word Bank

bury
clothe
corporal
feed
hungry
mercy
shepherd
shelter
sick
thirsty
visit
works

S	H	E	L	T	E	R	N	M	O
H	V	M	C	L	O	T	H	E	B
E	Y	C	R	E	M	K	C	I	S
P	F	H	Y	R	G	N	U	H	K
H	X	E	L	P	N	V	J	M	R
E	X	T	E	E	B	U	R	Y	O
R	Y	R	V	D	B	A	H	Z	W
D	P	M	V	I	S	I	T	D	C
X	Q	L	A	R	O	P	R	O	C
Y	W	J	T	H	I	R	S	T	Y

We Find Ways to Follow the Good Shepherd

Jesus asks us to follow him. We do this when we do good things for others. The Corporal Works of Mercy tell us some good things we can do.

Read the following letter that a fourth grader wrote to her parents. Underline the sentences in the letter that show how she followed the Good Shepherd.

Dear Mom and Dad,

I'm having a great time visiting with Aunt Marge! On Monday we went to a soup kitchen. We served lunch to some people who were hungry. I was glad that we could have pizza for supper that night.

The next day I helped Aunt Marge sort some clothes to give to the St. Vincent de Paul Society. The society will give the clothes to people who need them.

We've done a lot of visiting too. We went to see Great-aunt Lucy. She has been in a nursing home since she had a stroke. We also visited a museum to see the dinosaurs. They were awesome!

One day we helped to paint an apartment. People use it to shelter families who are homeless.

Each night Aunt Marge reminds me to pray for the people we help. She says to ask God to give them the gift of hope. I can't wait to get home and see you all again.

Love,

Julie

We Make a Stained-Glass Window of a Saint

All the faithful belong to the Communion of Saints. The saints in heaven and the souls in purgatory belong to the Communion of Saints. We pray to Mary and the saints.

In the space below draw and color a stained-glass window of a saint. You might draw the saint after whom you have been named or the saint after whom your parish has been named. You might draw your favorite saint!

We Discover a Bible Quote About Jesus and the Church

Jesus, the Son of God, founded the Church. When he preached the good news, some people did not believe him. They turned away from him and his message.

Solve this puzzle about Jesus and the Church. Use your math skills and the number code below to solve the puzzle.

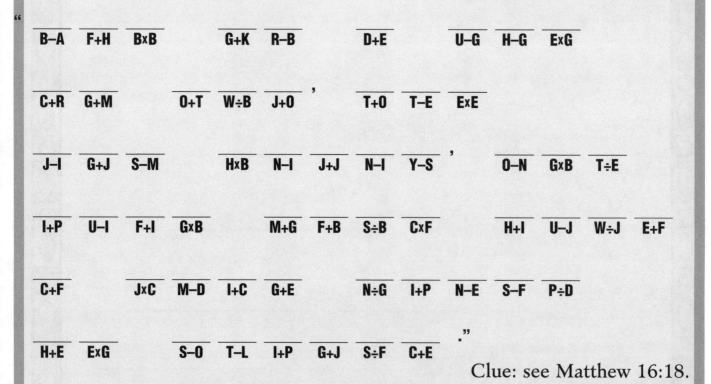

A	B	C	D	E	F	G	H	I	J	K	L	M	N	O	P	R	S	T	U	W	Y
1	2	3	4	5	6	7	8	9	10	11	12	13	14	15	16	17	18	20	25	30	35

"

B–A F+H BxB   G+K R–B   D+E   U–G H–G ExG

C+R G+M   O+T W÷B J+O '   T+O T–E ExE

J–I G+J S–M   HxB N–I J+J N–I Y–S '   O–N GxB T÷E

I+P U–I F+I GxB   M+G F+B S÷B CxF   H+I U–J W÷J E+F

C+F   JxC M–D I+C G+E   N÷G I+P N–E S–F P÷D

H+E ExG   S–O T–L I+P G+J S÷F C+E   ."

Clue: see Matthew 16:18.

We Match Liturgy Terms and Their Definitions

At the celebration of the liturgy, we gather to remember and share in God's work among us.

Match each liturgical term in Column A with its definition in Column B.

Liturgy Terms and Their Definitions

Column A	Column B
___1. liturgy	a. the season when we celebrate the birth of our Savior
___2. priest	b. the year-round celebration of the liturgical seasons and feasts
___3. Easter	c. the weeks of the liturgical year that are not Advent, Christmas, Lent, the Triduum, or Easter weeks
___4. Paschal Mystery	
___5. liturgical year	d. a time of expectation for Christ's coming
___6. Triduum	e. our season of preparation for Easter
___7. Advent	f. the Church's work of worshiping God
___8. Christmas	g. the season in which we celebrate that God raised Jesus to new life
___9. Lent	h. the leader of the worshiping assembly
___10. Ordinary Time	i. the name we give to God's plan of salvation
	j. the three-day celebration of Jesus' Paschal Mystery.

We Plan a Liturgical Prayer Service

Imagine that it is the Christmas season. With a partner or group of classmates, plan a prayer service to celebrate the birth of Jesus.

Follow the steps in the banner to help you plan your prayer service.

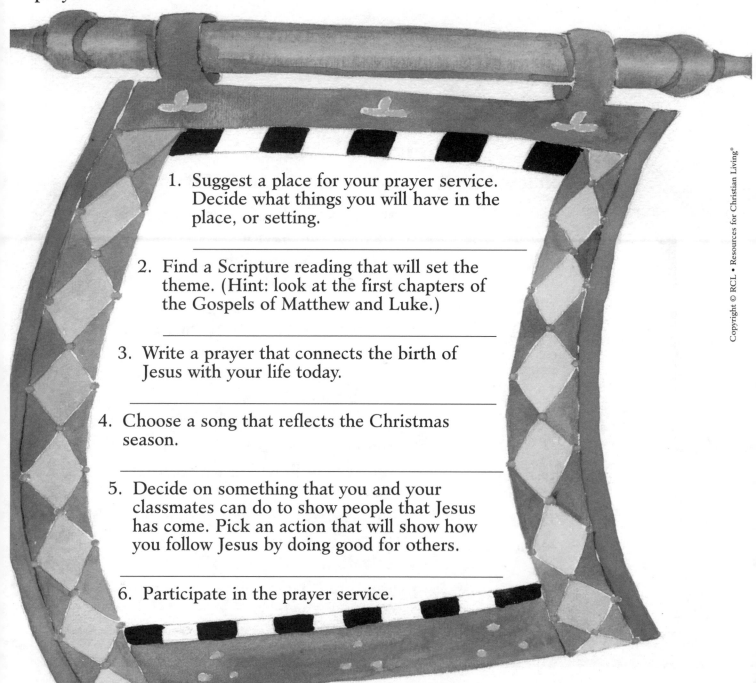

1. Suggest a place for your prayer service. Decide what things you will have in the place, or setting.

2. Find a Scripture reading that will set the theme. (Hint: look at the first chapters of the Gospels of Matthew and Luke.)

3. Write a prayer that connects the birth of Jesus with your life today.

4. Choose a song that reflects the Christmas season.

5. Decide on something that you and your classmates can do to show people that Jesus has come. Pick an action that will show how you follow Jesus by doing good for others.

6. Participate in the prayer service.

We Use Clues to Discover a Message About the Sacraments

The Church celebrates three Sacraments of Christian Initiation. These sacraments welcome us as members of the Church.

Use the following clues to complete the sentence below about one of the Sacraments of Christian Initiation.

Our Sacrament Message

1. The number before two is _____.

2. _____ rhymes with dove.

3. Subtract *y* from the word *they* and you get the word _____.

4. The seven main liturgical celebrations of the Church are called _____.

5. _____ rhymes with love.

6. Add *ian* to *Christ* and you get the word _____.

7. _____ is one step in joining a club or group.

8. Subtract *th* from the word *this* and you get the word _____.

9. The first sacrament we receive is _____.

1. __ __ __

2. __ __

3. __ __ __

4. __ __ __ __ __ __ __ __ __

5. __ __

6. __ __ __ __ __ __ __

7. __ __ __ __ __ __ __

8. __ __ __

9. __ __ __ __ __ __ __ __ __.

We Design a Place Mat for the Eucharist

The Eucharist is one of the Sacraments of Christian Initiation. In every celebration of the Eucharist, our Church family comes together to share the Eucharistic meal. We receive the Body and Blood of Christ.

In the outline, design a place mat that tells about the Eucharist. Draw pictures or make symbols for some or all of the following: bread, wine, table, stories, community, and Jesus' death and Resurrection.

Complete a Story About the Eucharist

Jesus once fed 5,000 people. He continues to feed us in the Eucharist. Each time we receive the Eucharist, we can remember this Bible story.

Use the words below to complete the story of how Jesus feeds us. Use the terms in the Word Bank to fill in the blanks of the story.

Word Bank

Nouns:

food   God   Israelites
Jesus   Last Supper
leftovers   loaves   manna
meal   memory

Verbs:

blessed   broke   cares
complained   gave

Adjectives:

five   twelve   two

The Eucharist

One day, more than _____ thousand people followed Jesus to a deserted place. _____ said to his disciples, "Give them some _____."

The disciples said: "Five _____ and _____ fish are all we have."

Jesus _____ and _____ the loaves and _____ them to the crowd. The _____ filled _____ baskets.

At the _____ _____, Jesus ate a final meal with his friends. He asked them to do this in _____ of him.

We trust that God always _____ for us. The Eucharist is a sacred _____. It recalls the time when the _____ escaped from Egypt. In the desert, they _____ to Moses. He asked _____ for help. God gave them _____. It looks like bread.

We Share with Others as Jesus Did

Christians care for others. With your classmates,
show that you care. Find a group of people to
help. Then have a collection to help them.

- Decide what your class or group will collect. You might collect food,
  clothing, toys, books, school supplies, or mittens.

- Decide on three things: a date for your collection, how to transport
  your items, and what kind of adult help you will need.

- Write an announcement for your collection activity. Tell people the
  what, why, where, when, who, and how of your collection. Write your
  announcement on this card.

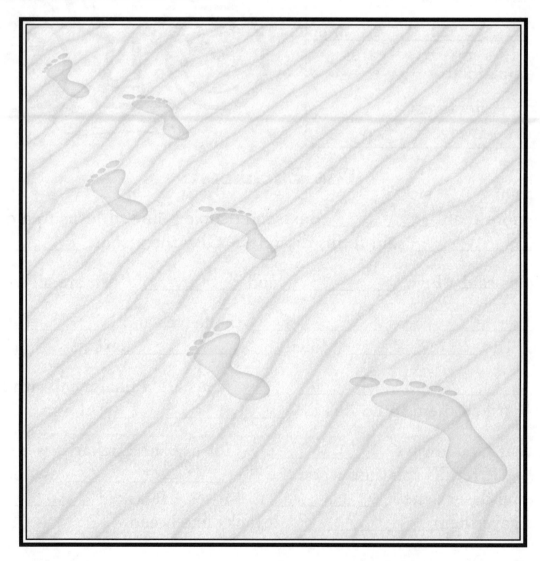

We Discover Jesus' Message About God's Love

The parable of the lost sheep tells us how much
God loves us.

Find Jesus' message from the parable of the Lost
Sheep. Fill in the missing vowels—a, e, i, o, u—in
the sentences below. Read Jesus' message.

Jesus' Message of Love

"'R_j___c_   w_th   m_   b_c___s_
__   h_v_   f___nd   my   l_st   sh___p.'
__   t_ll   y___,   _n   j_st   th_   s_m_
w_y   th_r_   w_ll   b_   m_r_   j_y
_n   h___v_n   _v_r   _n_   s_nn_r
wh_   r_p_nts   th_n   _v_r   n_n_ty—n_n_
r__ght_____s   p___pl_   wh_   h_v_   n_
n___d   _f   r_p_nt_nc__."

Clue: see Luke 15:6–7

We Create a Reconciliation Collage

God offers us forgiveness and reconciliation. We celebrate God's forgiving love in the sacrament of Reconciliation. In this space (or on large poster paper), create a collage of pictures, words, and drawings that show the need for healing and forgiveness. You might also show forgiveness and healing taking place. Share your collage with your class or group.

We Make Up a Story About Healing

In the Gospel according to Luke we read a story about Jesus healing a young girl. This story gives us hope. It helps us trust God's love.

Review pages 129–134 in your *Faith First Legacy* textbook. Find the words that rhyme with the clues below. Fill in the blanks with the rhyming words.

Rhyming Words about Healing

1. When people were sick, Jesus would _____, which rhymes with <u>seal</u>.

2. God created us to share his _____, which rhymes with <u>dove</u>.

3. We cheer people when we send them a _____, which rhymes with <u>hard</u>.

4. Jairus showed a great deal of _____, which rhymes with <u>crust</u>.

5. When we hear that someone is sick, we can always _____, which rhymes with <u>play</u>.

In the box, use some of the 5 words to tell your own story about healing.

Name _____

We Create Cards for People Who Are Sick

In the Gospel story, Jairus's daughter was sick. People tried to help her feel better. Then Jesus came and cured her. When people are sick, we can help them too. One way we help is by sending greeting cards.

Create a greeting card to send to someone who is sick.

On your card include a drawing and a happy message. When you are finished, cut out your card and fold it along the dotted line. (You might want to glue it to sturdy construction paper.) Now it is ready to be sent!

We Discover Our Domestic Church

Matrimony is a Sacrament at the Service of Communion. When a baptized man and a baptized woman marry, they answer God's call to have a family. The Christian family is called the domestic church. Your family teaches you about God.

Here are some questions to ask of yourself and the members of your family. The answers will show how your family helps you to learn about God.

My Domestic Church Questions

1. When does your family pray together? _____
   _____

2. What prayers do you usually pray? _____
   _____

3. Where do you keep your family Bible? _____
   _____

4. What crosses or pictures of Jesus, Mary, and the saints might you have in your house? _____
   _____

5. What does your family do to show God's love to those who have less than your family has? _____
   _____

6. What are some of your family traditions for Advent, Christmas, Lent, and Easter? _____
   _____

We Match Ten Terms About the Sacraments of Service

Holy Orders and Matrimony are the Sacraments at the Service of Communion.

The scrambled words in Column A are about the Sacraments at the Service of Communion. Unscramble each word and match it with its definition in Column B.

Sacraments at the Service of Communion Terms

Column A

1. linoHess

2. lyHo sredOr

3. conaseD

4. shiBop

5. erviceS

6. leRisougi

7. sirPha

8. muConitym

9. yFilam

10. trymaniMo

Column B

a. The sacrament that unites a baptized man and a baptized woman in a lifelong bond _____

b. The sacrament in which a man is consecrated to serve the Church _____

c. Christians who live in community and serve the Church _____

d. Men who may be married and are ordained to help bishops and priests _____

e. A group of people who live in one area and work together _____

f. The domestic church _____

g. Life in communion with God _____

h. Matrimony and Holy Order are Sacraments at the _____ of Communion.

i. Our local Church _____

j. Lays his hands on heads of men being ordained _____

We Decode a Message About God and Ourselves

The Book of Genesis in the Bible tells us the story of creation. It tells us why every person is important.

Using the code below, decode the Bible verse to discover why every person is important.

The Code

| A | B | C | D | E | F | G | H | I | J | K | L | M |
| N | O | P | Q | R | S | T | U | V | W | X | Y | Z |

Our Bible Message

Clue: see Genesis 1:27

We Write a Letter to God

God has given us many gifts. God has created us with an intellect, a free will, and emotions.

Write a thank-you letter to God. Tell God how thankful you are for one or all of these gifts. Explain why you are thankful. Tell God how you will use your gifts of intellect, free will, or emotions for the good of yourself and others.

Dear God,

We Use a Dot Detector to Discover a Beatitude

Jesus teaches us about happiness in the Beatitudes. In each of the Beatitudes, he describes one thing people do that leads to happiness.

Use the dot detector below to find one Beatitude that leads to happiness. Start with the first column. Then go across from left to right, copying the letters on the lines below. The first letter has been done for you.

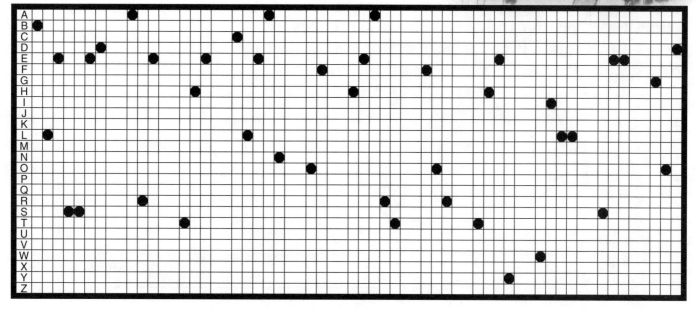

A Beatitude

B _ _ _ _ _ _ _   _ _ _   _ _ _   _ _ _ _ _

_ _   _ _ _ _ _,   _ _ _   _ _ _ _   _ _ _ _

_ _ _   _ _ _.

Clue: see Matthew 5:8

We Make a Beatitude Poem

When we live the Beatitudes, we find happiness. Use each letter in the word *Beatitude* to make a poem about happiness. Note that each line of the poem will begin with a letter in the word *Beatitude*.

Here is an example of a poem using the letters in the word Home.

> **H**ere in my room
> **O**n the second floor, I
> **M**eet a dinosaur
> **E**ach night in my favorite book!

The "Home" poem has only one sentence. Your "Beatitude" poem can have as many sentences as you want. Decide if you want to work with a partner or a group. Then write your "Beatitude" poem!

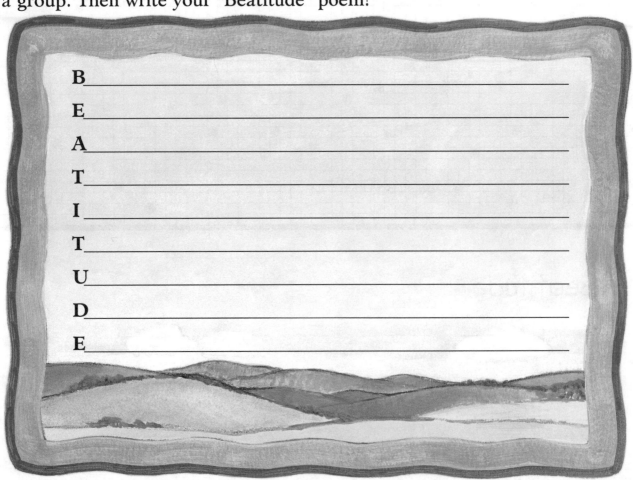

B_____

E_____

A_____

T_____

I_____

T_____

U_____

D_____

E_____

We Choose to Live a Moral Life and Follow Jesus

Each day we try to become better followers of
Jesus. We try to make good choices.

Think of your week ahead. In the spaces below
write what you will do next week to show that you
follow Jesus. Write how you will lead a holy life.

I Will Follow Jesus

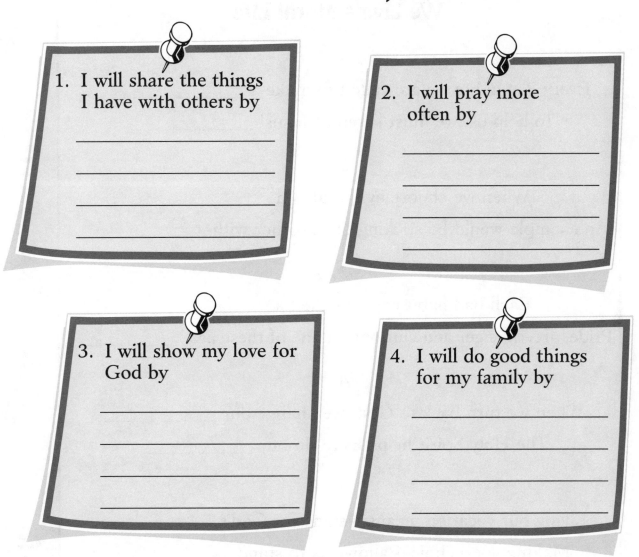

1. I will share the things
   I have with others by

   _____

   _____

   _____

2. I will pray more
   often by

   _____

   _____

   _____

3. I will show my love for
   God by

   _____

   _____

   _____

4. I will do good things
   for my family by

   _____

   _____

   _____

We Choose Rhyming Words About Living a Moral Life

God calls us to holiness. That is our vocation. Chapter 19 of your *Faith First Legacy* textbook tells you about choosing to live our call to holiness.

Finish the sentences below that sum up Chapter 19. The last word in each pair of sentences will rhyme. To make the rhymes, read the sentences well and go back and review Chapter 19.

vice

sin

heart

call

choice

We Live a Moral Life

1.

Every day in life we are called to make a _____.

To help us, we must listen to Jesus' _____.

2.

When we choose evil, that is a _____.

An example would be sticking our brother with a _____.

3.

Each bad habit can be called a _____.

Pride, greed, anger and gluttony—none of these are _____.

4.

When we turn back to God, we change our _____.

The Holy Spirit helps us to do our _____.

5.

Living our vocation means we answer God's _____.

Making good choices allows us to stand _____.

tall

voice

pin

part

nice

We Remember God's Laws of Love

God gave the Israelites the Ten Commandments to help them live good lives. These Commandments helped them make good choices.

Review the Ten Commandments on page 176 of your *Faith First Legacy* textbook. Then, with your book closed, fill in the missing words below.

The Ten Commandments

1. I am the Lord your _____. You shall not have strange _____ before me.

2. You shall not take the _____ of the Lord your _____ in vain.

3. Remember to keep _____ the Lord's day.

4. _____ your father and your mother.

5. You shall not _____.

6. You _____ not commit adultery.

7. You shall not _____.

8. You shall not bear _____ witness against your _____.

9. You shall not covet _____ neighbor's wife.

10. You shall not _____ your neighbor's goods.

Based on Exodus 20:2–17

We Create a Storyboard About Slavery and Freedom

The Israelites were slaves in Egypt. The Book of Exodus in the Bible tells how God freed them.

Create a four-part storyboard of the Israelites' journey from Egypt, or draw the story of someone who needs freedom today. Use speech bubbles to show what your characters are saying. When you are finished, share your story with your class or group.

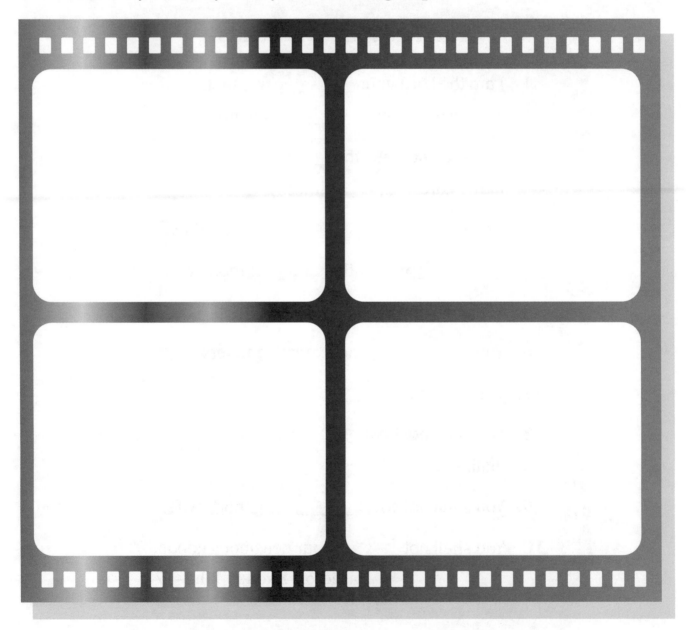

Name _____

We Find Words About the First Three Commandments

The First, Second, and Third Commandments help us honor God and show our love for God.

Look at the words in the Word Bank. They are words that describe the first three Commandments.

Find the words in the block of letters. Hint: the words may be horizontal, vertical, diagonal, backward, or forward.

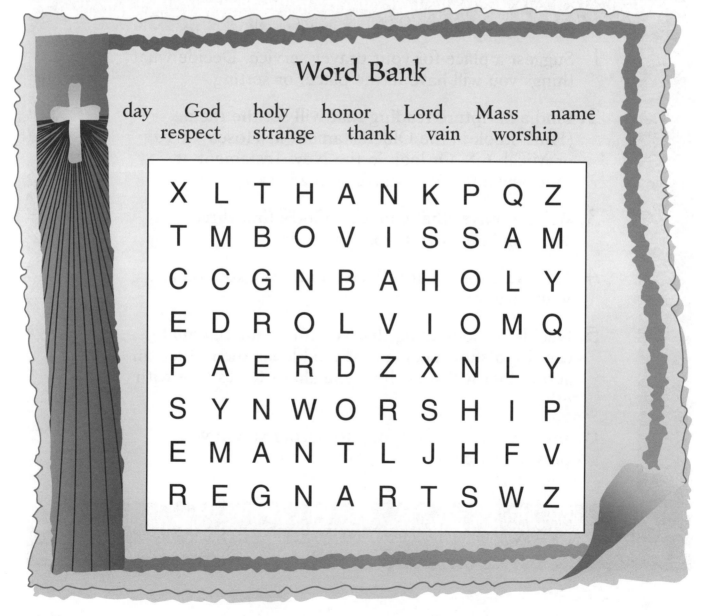

Word Bank

day   God   holy   honor   Lord   Mass   name
respect   strange   thank   vain   worship

```
X L T H A N K P Q Z
T M B O V I S S A M
C C G N B A H O L Y
E D R O L V I O M Q
P A E R D Z X N L Y
S Y N W O R S H I P
E M A N T L J H F V
R E G N A R T S W Z
```

We Plan a Commandment Prayer Service

The first three Commandments help us honor and respect God. With a partner or group of classmates, plan a prayer service to help you celebrate these Commandments.

Follow these steps to help you plan.

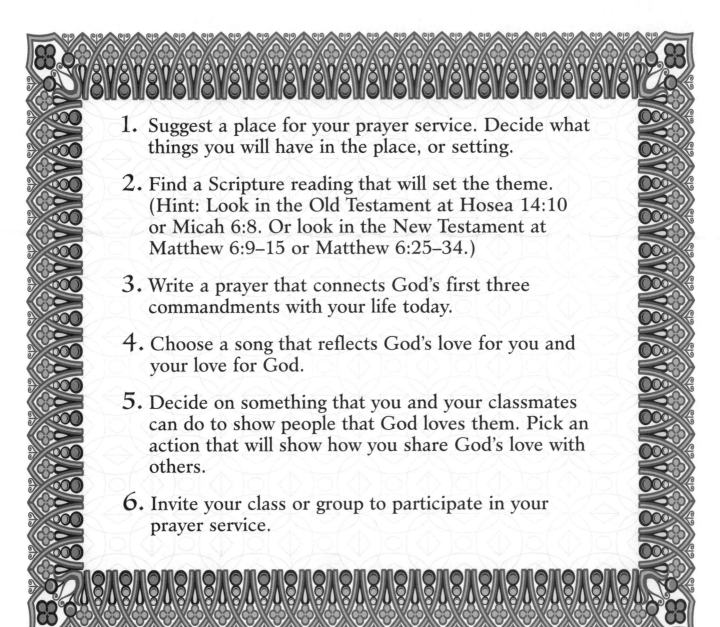

1. Suggest a place for your prayer service. Decide what things you will have in the place, or setting.

2. Find a Scripture reading that will set the theme. (Hint: Look in the Old Testament at Hosea 14:10 or Micah 6:8. Or look in the New Testament at Matthew 6:9–15 or Matthew 6:25–34.)

3. Write a prayer that connects God's first three commandments with your life today.

4. Choose a song that reflects God's love for you and your love for God.

5. Decide on something that you and your classmates can do to show people that God loves them. Pick an action that will show how you share God's love with others.

6. Invite your class or group to participate in your prayer service.

We Write a Play About Lazarus and the Rich Man

On page 191 of your *Faith First Legacy* textbook you learned about the Fifth Commandment. Look in the last paragraph and recall three ways that Jesus taught us to live this Commandment.

With a partner or a group of classmates, write a one-act play about this story.

- In Scene 1 show one friend making peace with another after an argument.

- In Scene 2 show a person who makes a good choice not to act on his or her feelings of anger toward someone else.

- In Scene 3 show someone who decides to show forgiveness to someone who has hurt him or her intentionally.

Create roles for several classmates. Think about using a narrator to tell part of the story.

Write dialogue for your characters to say. With this dialogue show what each character in the play is feeling and thinking.

Write stage directions too. Then the actors will know what hand gestures, facial expressions, and body movements they should use.

Finally, collect props, such as clothing that the actors can use to make your play seem more real.

With the help of some of your classmates, perform your play for your class or group.

Name _____

We Form a Community That Follows the Commandments

God gave us the Ten Commandments to help us live at peace with God, others, and ourselves.

Imagine that you and your classmates are going to form a Ten Commandments Community. With a partner or a group of classmates, think about what you need to do. Then answer the following questions:

Our Ten Commandments Community

1. What rules will we need to help us get along together?

2. Where will we set up this community and live?

3. What things will we share?

4. What will we have to give up to live in peace with each other?

5. How does living in a community help us follow Jesus?

After answering these questions, create a short prayer to ask God's help for your community.

_____

_____

_____

We Study Jesus' Words in the Bible

The Gospel according to John tells us what Jesus told his disciples about showing their love for others.

Fill in the missing vowels: a, e, i, o, u.

Discover what Jesus told us about love.

Jesus' Words

"Th __ s __ s my c __ mm __ ndm __ nt: l __ v __

__ n __ __ n __ th __ r __ s __ l __ v __ y __ __ .

N __ __ n __ h __ s gr __ __ t __ r l __ v __ th __ n

th __ s, t __ l __ y d __ wn __ n __ 's l __ f __ f __ r

__ n __ 's fr __ __ nds. Y __ __ __ r __ my fr __ __ nds

__ f y __ __ d __ wh __ t __ c __ mm __ nd y __ __ ."

Clue: see John 15:12–14.

We Learn from the Saints

The lives of the saints remind us how to live Jesus' commandment of love. Many of us are named after saints. Some of us have a favorite saint. These saints can teach us how to live Jesus' command.

Look up the life of a saint in a book about saints, in an encyclopedia, or on the Internet. Then write a paragraph about your saint. In your paragraph explain what your saint teaches you about how to live Jesus' command to love.

Copyright © RCL • Resources for Christian Living®

Name _____

We Solve a Prayer Crossword Puzzle

We can pray at any time and in any place. We can offer our work and our play to God.

Today, tell God about the fun you have as you work this crossword puzzle about prayer. Use the clues below, to complete the puzzle.

Our Prayer Crossword Puzzle

Across

3. _____ is the raising of our minds and hearts to God.

4. Celebrating the _____ is the main form of the prayer of the Church.

5. We pray to _____ the Father.

6. The liturgical year is divided into _____.

8. We profess our faith in the Apostles' _____.

10. Jesus taught his followers, or _____, how to pray.

Down

1. On the third day, Jesus was _____ from the dead.

2. In prayer, we give thanks and _____.

7. We pray the Apostles' and the _____ Creeds.

9. Every day, the Church prays the Liturgy of the _____.

We Rewrite the Nicene Creed

We profess our faith in the Nicene Creed. This creed tells others what we believe. Find the Nicene Creed on page 284 of your *Faith First Legacy* textbook. Read the creed together as a class or group.

Then divide into groups of three. Select one student to be the recorder for your group. In the scroll, write a creed about what the Church believes.

Afterward, read your creed to your classmates. Cut out the scroll, roll it up, put a ribbon around it, and place it on your prayer table.

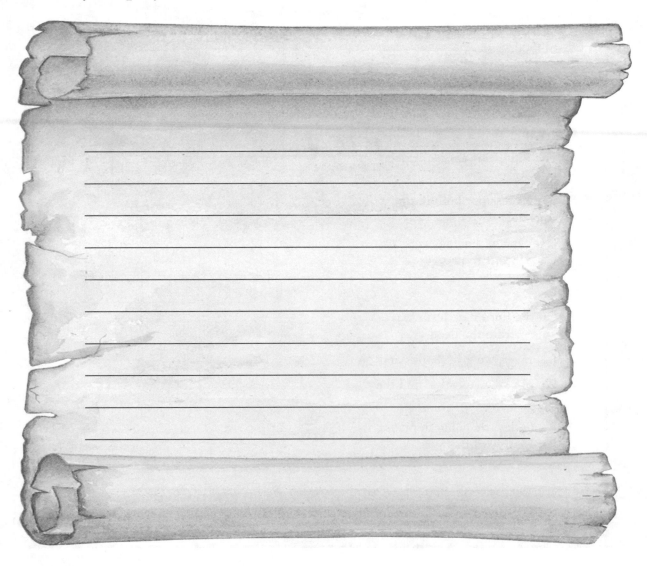

Name

We Decode a Message About Prayer

We pray in many ways. Every kind of prayer we pray is a sign that we believe and trust in God.

Find the ways we pray. Darken all the squares that contain the following letters: F, J, M, Q, U, V, W, X, Y, Z. The remaining words will be the answer to our puzzle.

F	Z	B	L	E	S	S	I	N	G	Q	W
W	X	Z	A	N	D	F	J	M	U	W	Y
A	D	O	R	A	T	I	O	N	M	J	W
T	H	A	N	K	S	G	I	V	I	N	G
W	Q	M	P	E	T	I	T	I	O	N	Y
Z	F	M	J	U	V	W	X	Y	Z	M	J
I	N	T	E	R	C	E	S	S	I	O	N

We Write a Praise Poem

We praise God for his mighty deeds. We tell God how good and wonderful he is. God blesses each of us.

Use each letter in the word *Praise* to make a poem to praise God. Note that each line of the poem will begin with a letter of the word *Praise*.

Here is an example of a poem made from the letters in the word *Prayer*.

Praise God all you
Rhinoceroses
And
You
Elephants!
Rejoice and
     be glad!

Decide if you want to work with a partner or a group. Then write your "Praise" poem!

P
R
A
I
S
E

Name _____

We Make a Web Page About Our Daily Bread

In the Our Father, we pray "Give us this day our daily bread." If we are hungry, that bread can be food to eat. But what if we are lonely? Then our daily bread might be a friend. What if we are angry? Then our daily bread might be peace and reconciliation. Our daily bread is anyone or anything that we need to live as children of God.

Think of people in your neighborhood or around the world who need "daily bread." Create a web page that shows how God can give us our daily bread—whatever that bread may be. Decorate your page in a way that will attract visitors. Spread the Good News! Live the Our Father!

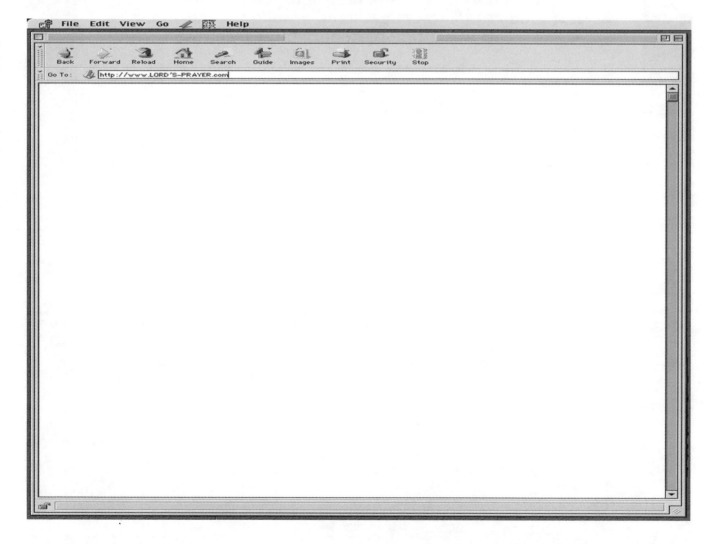

Name _____

We Find Words About Jesus and Prayer

Jesus often prayed and taught his disciples to pray. The Holy Spirit, our parents, our teachers, and the Church teach us to pray.

Chapter 26 in your *Faith First Legacy* textbook teaches you about prayer. Below are five riddles. Use the clues in each riddle to discover a person or word mentioned in Chapter 26. Write each answer on the line provided.

Words About Jesus and Prayer

1.
This is a wise and holy person of biblical times.
A group of followers gathered around this person.
This was a title of honor and respect.

_____

2.
They followed Jesus.
They trusted him to help them understand God's Law.
They listened, watched, and questioned Jesus.

_____

3.
This is a prayer Jesus taught us.
His disciples asked Jesus to teach them to pray.
We still pray this prayer at Mass.

_____

4.
These words say what we need each day.
We can help others receive this through our kindness.
This can be food or acts of kindness.

_____

5.
This is a prayer of praise.
We pray this prayer at Mass.
We conclude the Our Father with this prayer.

_____

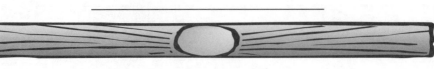

We Find Words from the Liturgical Year

We call the Church's year the liturgical year. Each box below contains one syllable of a word from the Church's year. Look at the syllables. Put the numbers of the syllable boxes together to form the words. The first word (Advent) has been done for you. It is made up of the syllables from boxes 6 and 9. Share your answers with your class or group.

1 Or	2 Pen	3 Time	4 um	5 cal	6 Ad
7 Sun	8 Christ	9 vent	10 Fri	11 Palm	12 u
13 Eas	14 Trid	15 Lent	16 day	17 di	18 tur
19 cost	20 nar	21 Li	22 ter	23 te	24 Good
25 gi	26 The	27 Year	28 day	29 mas	30 y

Advent	6 and 9	Ordinary Time	_____
Christmas	_____	Palm Sunday	_____
Easter	_____	Pentecost	_____
Good Friday	_____	The Liturgical Year	_____
Lent	_____	Triduum	_____

We Act Out an Advent Play

During Advent we listen to a Gospel story about John the Baptist. He helped people get ready for the coming of Jesus.

With your classmates, act out the following play about John the Baptist. You will need four actors, or characters.

John Prepares for the Coming of Jesus

Narrator: We are at the Jordan River. A man named John is baptizing all who come to him. A man and a woman from a nearby village stand on the banks of the river.

Aaron: I want to go into the water and be baptized with the others.

Hester: I'm not sure. He looks strange to me. He's wearing animal skins, and they say he eats bugs.

Aaron: Yes, but he says that we need to prepare the way of the Lord.

Hester: I need to prepare dinner!

John the Baptist: I baptize you with water. But believe me—someone is coming who is mightier than I am! He will baptize you with the Holy Spirit and with fire.

Aaron: Don't you see? We must repent and make ourselves ready for the Messiah!

Hester: John's faith has set me on fire! I want to get ready for the Messiah too!

Narrator: The two villagers approach John, bow their heads, and ask him to baptize them. Smiling, they step into the river.

-The End-

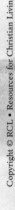

We E-Mail a New Friend About the Birth of Jesus

Many rejoiced when Jesus was born. Every Christmas people continue to rejoice because of the birth of Jesus.

But even today, there are people all over the world who have not heard the Christmas story. Be an "e-mail missionary"!

On the computer screen, compose an e-mail telling the Christmas story. Be sure to explain why Christmas is so important for all people.

We Make True Statements About Lent

During Lent we prepare ourselves to celebrate Easter. To help you get ready, study the sentences below. Write true if the statement is true. Write false if the statement is not true. Then make each false statement true by changing the underlined word or words.

Our Lenten Statements

1. Lent is the Church's <u>winter</u>.

   _____

2. On Ash <u>Sunday</u> the priest traces the Sign of the Cross on our forehead with ashes.

   _____

3. The priest says "Turn away from sin and be faithful to the <u>Gospel</u>."

   _____

4. Lent is the season of the Church's year that reminds us to <u>forgive</u> others and to ask for forgiveness.

   _____

5. During Lent many people receive the sacrament of <u>Ordination</u>.

   _____

6. The early Christians learned from Jesus. So they went to the Temple or they gathered in their home to <u>pray</u>.

   _____

7. The Church's daily prayer is called the Liturgy of the <u>People</u>.

   _____

8. During Lent many people <u>fast</u>, or give up things.

   _____

9. On the night before he died, Jesus offered his followers the gift of <u>peace</u>.

   _____

10. Pope Paul VI said, "If you want peace, work for <u>prudence</u>."

    _____

We Write a Triduum Poem

The Triduum is the last three days of Holy Week. The days that make up the celebration of the Triduum are Holy Thursday, Good Friday, and Easter. During these days we celebrate God's love for us. We rejoice in God's goodness to us. We praise God for raising Jesus from the dead.

Use each letter in the word *Triduum* to make a poem. Note that each line of the poem will begin with a letter in the word *Triduum*.

Here is an example of a poem made from the letters in the word *Easter*.

Each year we
Are happy when we
See lilies all white and blooming on
The altar.
Each year we
Rejoice!

Your "Triduum" poem will have two lines that begin with the letter U. You may want to work with a partner or a group.

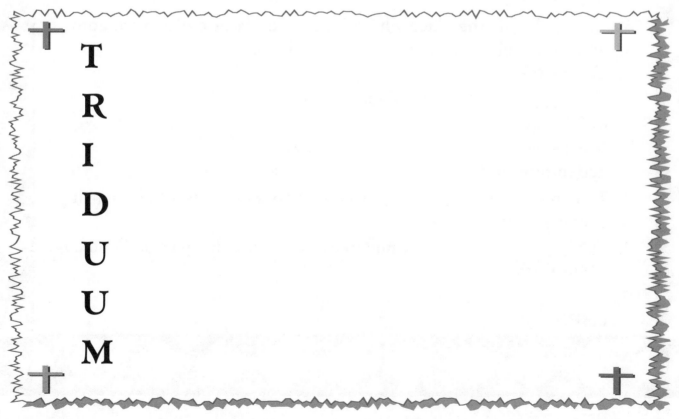

T
R
I
D
U
U
M

We Unscramble Easter and Pentecost Words

Rejoice! God has raised Jesus to new life! The words
below the sentences are related to Easter and
Pentecost. Read the definitions. Then unscramble each
word and write it on the line to complete the sentence.

We Celebrate Easter!

1. _____ is an expression of praise.
   ullleiAa

2. _____ is a song of joy.
   tuxlEte

3. _____ is a Hebrew word for peace.
   ahlomS

4. Jesus' _____ is the reason we celebrate Easter.
   notrusRerice

5. _____ is the place where Jesus and his disciples were going
   when he explained the Scriptures to them.
   aEmmsu

6. _____ is the name given to a follower of Jesus.
   aiiChnrst

7. Jesus gave us a new _____ of love.
   acdemmmnnot

8. The apostles were _____ to the events of Jesus' life on earth.
   eeeeinssstwy

9. The _____ _____ came to Mary and the disciples on Pentecost.
   iiHloprSty

10. _____ is the way we bless and thank God.
    aeiPrs

Answer Key

Chapter 1

We Find a Message of Faith
"My Lord and my God"

We Believe That God Will Always Be With Us
1. God
2. Faith
3. Creeds

Chapter 2

We Learn About the Covenant
"Everything the Lord has said, we will do."

Chapter 3

We Unscramble Words From a Bible Story
1. Hannah
2. Samuel
3. Shrine
4. Israelites
5. Ark of the Covenant
6. Shiloh
7. Judges
8. Old Testament
9. Jerusalem
10. Temple

Chapter 5

We Discover a Promise God Made
"My love shall never leave you."

Chapter 6

We Know That Jesus Wants Us to Have Faith
"Let it be done for you according to your faith."

Chapter 7

We Put Events in Jesus' Life in the Order They Happened

1 = e	6 = j
2 = h	7 = f
3 = a	8 = c
4 = g	9 = i
5 = b	10 = d

Chapter 8

We Solve a Pentecost Crossword Puzzle

Across	Down
2. Pentecost	1. Jesus
4. wind	3. Trinity
5. Spirit	6. promised
7. fire	9. God
8. symbols	10. faith
11. courage	

CHAPTER 9

We Unscramble Words About a Bible Story

We Find Ways to Follow the Good Shepherd

The following should be underlined:
- Served lunch to people who were hungry
- Helped sort some clothes to give to the St. Vincent de Paul Society
- Visited Great-aunt Lucy
- Helped paint an apartment

Chapter 10

We Discover a Bible Quote About Jesus and the Church
"And so I say to you, you are Peter, and upon this rock I will build my church."

CHAPTER 11

We Match Liturgy Terms and Their Definitions

1 = f	6 = j
2 = h	7 = d
3 = g	8 = a
4 = i	9 = e
5 = b	10 = c

Chapter 12

We Use Clues to Discover a Message About the Sacraments
One of the Sacraments of Christian Initiation is Baptism.

Chapter 13

Complete a Story about the Eucharist
One day, more than **five** thousand people followed Jesus to a deserted place. **Jesus** said to his disciples, "Give them some **food**." The disciples said: "Five **loaves** and **two** fish are all we have." Jesus **blessed** and **broke** the loaves and **gave** them to the crowd. The **leftovers** filled **twelve** baskets. At the **Last Supper**, Jesus ate a final meal with his friends. He asked them to do this in **memory** of him. We trust that God always **cares** for us. The Eucharist is a sacred **meal**. It recalls the time when the **Israelites** escaped from Egypt. In the desert, they **complained** to Moses. He asked **God** for help. God gave them **manna**. It looks like bread.

Chapter 14

We Discover Jesus' Message About God's Love
"'Rejoice with me because I have found my lost sheep.' I tell you, in just the same way there will be more joy in heaven over one sinner who repents than over ninety-nine righteous people who have no need of repentance."

Chapter 15

We Make Up a Story about Healing
1. heal
2. love
3. card
4. trust
5. pray

Answer Key

Chapter 16

We Match Ten Terms About the Sacraments of Service

1. Holiness = g
2. Holy Orders = b
3. Deacons = d
4. Bishop = j
5. Service = h
6. Religious = c
7. Parish = i
8. Community = e
9. Family = f
10. Matrimony = a

Chapter 17

We Decode a Message About God and Ourselves

God created man in his image; in the divine image he created him; male and female he created them.

Chapter 18

We Use a Dot Detector to Discover a Beatitude

"Blessed are the clean of heart, for they will see God."

Chapter 19

We Choose Rhyming Words About Living a Moral Life

1. choice; voice
2. sin; pin
3. vice; nice
4. heart; part
5. call; tall

Chapter 20

We Remember God's Laws of Love

1. I am the Lord your **God**. You shall not have strange **gods** before me.
2. You shall not take the **name** of the Lord your **God** in vain.
3. Remember to keep **holy** the Lord's Day.
4. **Honor** your father and your mother.
5. You shall not **kill**.
6. You **shall** not commit adultery.
7. You shall not **steal**.

8. You shall not bear **false** witness against your **neighbor**.
9. You shall not covet **your** neighbor's wife.
10. You shall not **covet** your neighbor's goods.

CHAPTER 21

We Find Words About the First Three Commandments

Chapter 23

We Study Jesus' Words in the Bible

"This is my commandment: love one another as I love you. No one has greater love than this, to lay down one's life for one's friends. You are my friends if you do what I command you."

Chapter 24

We Solve a Prayer Crossword Puzzle

Across
3. prayer
4. Liturgy
5. God
6. seasons
8. ~~creed~~ rose
10. apostles

Down
1. ~~raised~~ creed
2. praise
7. Nicene
9. hours

Chapter 25

We Decode a Message About Prayer

Blessing and Adoration, Thanksgiving, Petition, Intercession

CHAPTER 26

We Find Words About Jesus and Prayer

1. Teacher
2. Disciples
3. Lord's Prayer
4. Daily Bread
5. Doxology

The Liturgical Year

We Find Words from the Liturgical Year

Advent 6 and 9
Christmas 8 and 29
Easter 13 and 22
Good Friday 24, 10 and 16 or 28
Lent 15
Ordinary Time 1, 17, 20, 30 and 3
Palm Sunday 11, 7 and 16 or 28
Pentecost 2, 23 and 19
The Liturgical Year 26, 21, 18, 25, 5 and 27
Triduum 14, 12 and 4

Lent

We Make True Statements About Lent

1. False—spring
2. False—Wednesday
3. True
4. True
5. False—Reconciliation
6. True
7. False—Hours
8. True
9. True
10. False—justice

Easter

We Unscramble Easter and Pentecost Words

1. Alleluia
2. Exultet
3. Shalom
4. Resurrection
5. Emmaus
6. Christian
7. commandment
8. eyewitnesses
9. Holy Spirit
10. Praise